NOVEL REVISION PROMPTS

by Rayne Hall

NOVEL REVISION PROMPTS

Rayne Hall

Book cover by Erica Syverson and Uros Jovanovic

Interior Illustrations by Marvin Alonso, Srijit, Hanna-Riikka

© 2016 Rayne Hall (text and images)

March 2016 Edition

CONTENTS

INTRODUCTION

You've written a novel, and the draft brims with promise. Now you're revising it to shape it into a gripping work of fiction readers can't put down.

Revising a novel is fun. With each change, you see your book grow closer to your vision and gain more power.

In this book, I offer you sixty-eight ideas on how to bring out your novel's full potential. Play with them, experiment, explore where they'll lead.

To help you find the kind of prompts you need right now, I've sorted them into three groups:

- **Plot Revision**

  Use this section if you have a first draft – perhaps after completing a NaNoWriMo sprint – and want to shape it into a powerful, emotion-rousing book.

- **Scene Revision**

  Here you'll find ideas to transform dull, dragging scenes into riveting reads with tension and sizzle.

- **Line Editing**

  Before you indie-publish your book or submit it to agents, enhance your style with sharp writing and a strong voice, where every word pulls the reader in. The polishing prompts help make your book sparkle with diamond quality.

With many prompts, I'll provide tips on how you can put the idea into practice. Interpret them creatively and adapt them to suit your unique story. If you've already applied an idea, or if it isn't a good fit for your novel, skip to a different one. Pick the prompts that make you tingle with excitement.

When referring to the main character – who is usually the same person as the protagonist, point-of-view character and hero – I use the abbreviation MC. To avoid clunky 'he or she' constructions, I sometimes write 'he' and sometimes 'she'. The grammar, punctuation and spelling in this book are British English.

Now, let's have fun improving your book.

Rayne Hall

PLOT REVISION PROMPTS

Use this section if you have a first draft – perhaps after completing a NaNoWriMo sprint – and want to shape it into a powerful, emotion-rousing book.

PLOT REVISION PROMPT:
THE MC'S BIG SECRET

The main character has a secret. What is it?

He may have come to regret a mistake he made in his youth. Perhaps his work as an undercover agent requires him to hide his true identity. Or perhaps he keeps a secret to protect someone else.

What would be the disastrous consequences if someone discovered and revealed the truth? He might lose his career prospects or the respect of his community. The discovery might condemn him to a life sentence in prison, ruin the cause he's fighting for, or cause unbearable hurt to the one he loves.

What measures does he take to guard his secret? He may change the subject whenever the topic comes up, tell lies, change his name, wear a disguise, avoid people who might recognise him from his dark past.

When someone confronts him with the truth, what does he do? He may respond with angry denials, treat the suggestion as a joke, accuse the person of fabricating lies, or wrap himself in haughtiness and decline to react to such base allegations.

The further the plot progresses, the more entangled the pretence becomes. Even if he wanted to come clean, it's too late.

What if the MC decides (probably at the novel's climax) to end the deceit and confess all... including his previous lies?

PLOT REVISION PROMPT:
ADD AN ANIMAL CHARACTER

Readers like animal characters. Could your MC have an animal sidekick? What kind of animal is it?

This could be a 'normal' pet like a dog, cat or horse, or something unusual, such as a goat, ferret or camel. (What's normal or unusual, plausible or implausible, depends on the culture and the location – a dog would be an uncommon choice in a Muslim society, while in Britain it would be difficult to keep a camel.) If possible, choose a kind of animal you know well, so you can write about it with knowledge and authenticity. If you keep rats, give your MC a rat companion. If you love horse riding, let the special animal be a horse.

Do the MC and her animal already have an established bond at the beginning of the novel, or are they meeting for the first time? The initial encounter can serve to establish the MC's likeability (especially if she rescues the animal from harm) and warm the reader's heart.

Develop the animal as a real character, with likes, dislikes, interests and habits.

The animal needs to play an active role in the plot.

What if the villain kidnaps or threatens the animal to blackmail the MC? What if something unusual about the animal's behaviour alerts the MC to an unseen danger? What if the villain attacks the MC, and the animal leaps into the fight?

PLOT REVISION PROMPT:
WHAT'S THE GOAL, AND WHAT'S AT STAKE?

What does the MC want or need and try to achieve throughout the story? If you weren't aware of this goal while writing the draft, now is the time to identify it.

Does she need to find a good man to marry, or a serial killer to arrest? Is she questing for an ancient treasure, trying to solve the dark mystery of her past, or developing a cure for cancer?

Establish this goal as early as possible in your novel. Depending on the genre and the structure, you may be able to state the goal on the first page.

Why does she want to achieve this goal? Give her several reasons - some of which she shares in public, others are private and may even be secret. Some reasons are emotional, others rational. Some are selfish, others selfless.

Let's say the MC is a homicide detective. Her goal is to hunt down and arrest the serial killer who murders ten-year-old boys. Her cocktail of reasons: she wants to prevent more children dying, she wants justice, she wants to prove that a woman can do this job, she wants to get promoted within the homicide department, she wants to wipe that contemptuous smirk off her colleague's face, she wants to avenge the sweet neighbour boy who was the killer's first victim, she wants her town to be safe, she wants to feel a useful member of the police force, she wants her father to be proud of her.... that's nine.

Give your MC at least five reasons for what she wants, more if you can.

What's at stake? What would be the consequences of her failure?

In the case of the killer-hunting detective, these might include: more children would die, she would never gain her father's respect, families would move away from the town, her colleague would despise her, she would feel like a failure, and more.

Raise the stakes as high as possible, and remind your readers often what's at stake.

PLOT REVISION PROMPT: WORK YOUR THEME

What's your book's theme? You may have written the novel without a theme in mind, but now that the draft is complete, you can identify it.

The theme may be a moral – a message your reader walks away with, the lesson absorbed. Keep it to a simple statement, such as:

Love conquers all.
Good triumphs over evil.
Who dares, wins.

It could also be two virtuous values warring in the MC's mind. She holds both dear and tries to pursue them at the same time, but has to make tough decisions and sacrifice one for the other. This type of theme is based on the MC's inner conflict and works especially well in heart-wrenching novels and works with emotional depth.

Here are examples:

Honour versus loyalty.
Honesty versus love.
Justice versus peace.

Now you've chosen your theme, make the most of it. In what additional ways could you develop it in your novel?

Ideally, every scene should contribute to the theme, even if it's only in a small way. For example, if your theme is 'honour versus loyalty', you could tweak every scene so someone behaves either honourably or honestly in some way.

In crucial scenes – at the novel's turning points – it's worth milking the theme in a big way, for example by forcing the MC to choose between honesty and loyalty.

What if, during the novel's Black Moment, the opposite of the theme seems true? For instance, if the theme is 'good triumphs over evil', then evil triumphs during the Black Moment.

What if, during the novel's Black Moment or Climax scenes, the MC has to choose between her two values, sacrificing one for the other? For example, if the theme is 'honesty versus loyalty', she has to tell a lie in order to be loyal, or to be disloyal in order to serve the truth.

PLOT REVISION PROMPT:
WHAT WOULD THE MC NEVER DO?

Consider your MC's deeply held values, beliefs and principles. What would she never do?

For example, your MC is a deeply moral woman who disdains carnality and the one thing she would never do is practice prostitution.

Let her state this several times in the story in different ways. She may say, "I would never sell my body!" or she may make disdainful remarks about women who do.

What would have to happen to make her do the one thing she thinks she would never do? Obviously, these have to be unforeseen, drastic circumstances. Make them happen in your novel.

If your moral MC would never prostitute herself, put her in a situation where her children are starving, and the only way to put food on the table is to accept a wealthy man's offer for a night.

The MC forced to act against her deeply held values gives the readers a compelling story they cannot forget.

What if your MC would never tell a lie... and then has to lie to get out of a situation alive?

What if the villain forces her to do the one thing she would never willingly consent to?

What if she is a pacifist who would never use violence... and then she gets the chance to assassinate the dictator who is about to order a holocaust?

PLOT REVISION PROMPT: MAKE READERS LIKE YOUR MC FROM THE START

Let your MC do a good deed in the first scene, if possible on the first page. Ideally, he's protecting someone helpless, and he does it in a matter-of-course way, not making a big deal of it.

For best effect, let the person he helps be someone helpless who can't help themselves, and nobody else is making a move to to help. The MC takes the necessary action, then continues pursuing his goal.

This will only need a paragraph or so. Look at the opening scene, and consider whom he can help and in what way, without requiring major changes to the scene.

What if he sees a cat trapped under a car and frees it?
What if he witnesses a child getting bullied and intervenes?
What if he sees a man molesting a woman and steps in?
What if he aids a frail old lady walk down the stairs?
What if he helps a frightened old man cross a busy road?
What if he holds the door open for a wheelchair user?
What if he offers his seat to an exhausted mother?

If your MC has an animal companion, this can be a good way to introduce them. The MC rescues the animal, and the animal becomes his loyal companion.

PLOT REVISION PROMPT:
GIVE YOUR MC A DISABILITY

Readers root for characters with disability. Could your MC be physically disabled? If this doesn't work for the plot, perhaps one of the MC's allies could have a handicap.

If possible, write about what you know. Choose a disability you're familiar with, either because you live it or because someone you know well does. This allows you to write with plausibility and authenticity. You know what it's like and don't need to rely on your imagination and stereotypes.

Make the disability part of the plot. How does it hamper the character's pursuits?

What if she needs to make a quick getaway – but can't in her wheelchair?

What if she needs to enter a building which has no wheelchair ramp?

What if she knows the phone call is urgent and will save lives – but she can't hear, and nobody else is around?

What if she needs to find an object, and can't see, so she has to rely on touch for her search?

What if people are scared when seeing her malformed face?

What if she can't get a job because her constant muscle twitches make potential employers uncomfortable?

Readers cheer when a character uses a disability to advantage. Think of situations where you could make this happen as part of the plot.

What if she uses her crutch to hit the emergency off-switch nobody else can reach?

What if she uses her facial disfigurement to frighten the superstitious evil-doer into revealing what he's done?

What if several people are trapped in total darkness and panicking, while the blind MC moves with her usual confidence and finds a way out?

PLOT REVISION PROMPT:
WHAT DOES THE MC FEAR MOST?

What does our MC fear? Perhaps he worries about losing his professional licence, having his home repossessed, getting outed as gay, or his ex-wife winning custody of their kids. Maybe he's terrified of poverty, sickness or dishonour. He could have a phobia - what if he fears spiders, enclosed spaces, or heights?

Establish this fear on several occasions during the novel's first half. Then, in the second half, make it happen.

What if the villain knows the MC's dark secret and leaks it to the press?

What if the villain uses the MC's terror of snakes and throws him into a snake pit?

What if the hero has a phobia of heights, but the only way to rescue his little daughter is to climb down a steep cliff?

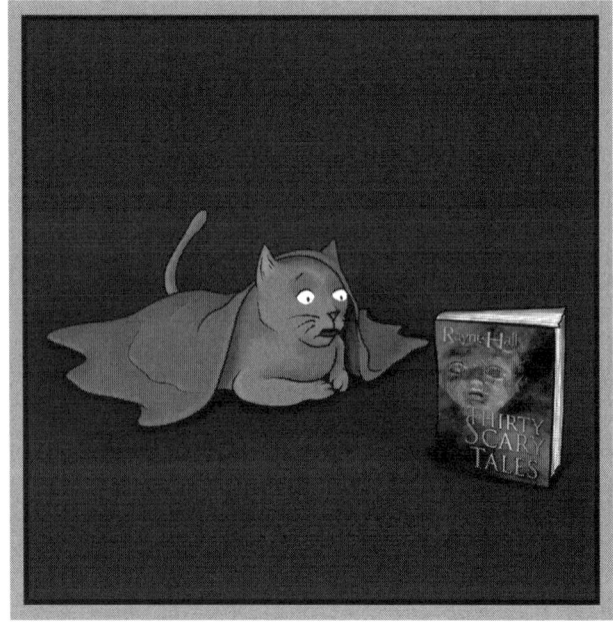

PLOT REVISION PROMPT:
WHAT PLACE DOES THE MC AVOID?

Is there a place your MC doesn't go to – a room, a building, a footpath, a landmark or a town? She has strong reasons, related perhaps to unhappy memories, troubling guilt, a promise, fear of getting recognised by locals, a phobia or a religious taboo.

In the first half of the novel, show her successfully avoiding the place. When a friend suggests a visit there, she offers an alternative destination. When relatives expect her attendance, she finds an excuse not to turn up. She may send a stand-in, get ill, lose her way or have a car breakdown – whatever will get her out of the need to enter that place.

Then in the second half, she is in the place she dreads, and an important part of the plot unfolds there, maybe even the Black Moment or the Climax.

What makes her go there after all her resistance? Think of a compelling reason.

Has she arrived there by accident, not realising where her lover was taking her?

Has the villain abducted her and imprisoned her there?

Is she deliberately trying to overcome her dislike of the place, attempting to disprove superstitions?

Is she trying to rescue someone who has ignored the danger warnings, entered the place and not come back?

Is someone blackmailing her – "if you want your daughter back unharmed, come to Gallows Hill at midnight."

Is she searching for the crucial clue to unravel the dark mystery of her past?

PLOT REVISION PROMPT:
TAKE AWAY THE ALLIES

Who are the MC's allies? Make a list of everyone who supports him or his cause: colleagues, friends, family, neighbours, consultants, clients, police officers, hired freelancers, counsellors, church members, fellow victims, old school mates and people who owe him favours.

During the MC's quest for the goal, he counts on their help, whether it's financial aid, information, access or moral support.

As the plot unfolds, take away one ally after the other, until the MC finds himself alone during the novel's Black Moment.

What if the most valued member of the expedition cries off in the last minute, citing family issues?

What if the hired guide steals the expedition's valuable equipment and vanishes, leaving them without local knowledge?

What if the bank that promised a loan for the venture reneges because someone planted false rumours about the MC?

What if the police officer on whom he counted to hunt down the serial killer turns against him, declaring him a suspect?

What if the MC falls out with his best mate who walks out of the project?

What if his assistant turns out to be an undercover agent for the opposition, sent to spy on him?

What if his fiancée tells him she has had enough of this dangerous lifestyle – either he gives up his pursuit, or she leaves... and she does?

What if the MC's second-in-command turns traitor and betrays the secret to the enemy?

What if he doesn't trust his most capable lieutenant's motivations?

What if his one absolutely loyal ally fights bravely for him against all odds – and dies, leaving the MC all alone?

PLOT REVISION PROMPT: SHORTENING THE BOOK

If your book is too long, condense the time frame. Does the draft follow two years of the MC's life? Condense it to one. Does it span fifteen years? Let the events happen in five. You'll be surprised how much shorter the resulting manuscript becomes. At the same time, the novel will gain in overall pace.

Pay attention to continuity, such as any mention of ages and anniversaries. Keep track of the seasons, so you don't have frost riming the windows in summer and two Christmas celebrations in one year.

Reduce the cast of characters. The resulting novel will not only be shorter, but gain depth.

If the MC has three sisters and two deputies, consider if one of each will do.

Combine several characters into one. Could the MC's sister also be his deputy? What if the nosy neighbour is also the villain's henchman? What if the homeless woman is also the fortune-teller? What if the school teacher is also the leader of the church choir?

PLOT REVISION PROMPT: EXPANDING THE BOOK

Would you like your novel to be longer, more complex, with greater emotional depth?

Add a subplot.

Weave the subplot around characters who already have a role in the novel, such as the MC's daughter and the villain's son.

A great subplot is related to the main plot. Consider the MC's goal. Could the subplot's focal character pursue a similar goal, but for different reasons and with different methods? Might the subplot character experience a different side of the same issue?

Let's say the MC's goal in the novel is to find his birth mother who gave him up for adoption. What if a subplot character is pregnant and considers adoption versus abortion? What if a childless couple is dealing with the legalities and ethical dilemmas of adopting a Third World child?

You can also weave the subplot around the story's theme or the MC's inner conflict.

If the main plot evolves around the theme 'love conquers all', let the subplot carry the same message, but exploring a different kind of love between different people in different circumstances.

If the MC has to make tough choices between loyalty and love, let the subplot character experience a dilemma between those values too, but with different priorities and outcomes. Where the MC is torn between loyalty to his family and love for his bride, the subplot character has to decide between loyalty to her country and love for her mother.

Subplots usually require a switch of Point-of-View for those scenes.

Which character in your novel might experience a dilemma that reflects an aspect of the MC's goal or shines a different light on the novel's theme?

PLOT REVISION PROMPT: CONNECT THE PROTAGONIST AND THE ANTAGONIST

Create a layer of emotional depth by connecting the protagonist (the MC) and the antagonist (the MC's opponent, who may be the story's villain). What do they have in common?

Are they siblings? Did they grow up in the same orphanage, attend the same school, love the same man? Do they share a passion for travel, organic gardening or horse racing? Did both lose their spouses to a drug overdose? Are both disabled and dependent on wheelchairs? Do both value courtesy as a virtue?

This commonality can add meaning, conflict and complexity without complicating your plot.

Decide what the two have in common. Then consider how this affects the story.

What if the villain knows the MC's secret, and leverages it to torment or to blackmail the MC?

What if sharing the antagonist's passion helps the heroine understand his psyche and allows her to target his vulnerability?

What if the MC needs to take action against the antagonist, but can't bring herself to because of their childhood bond?

PLOT REVISION PROMPT:
THE MC LEARNS A LESSON

During the novel, the MC grows in wisdom and maturity. He makes several mistakes and learns from them. One lesson is particularly harsh but effective, and changes his attitude and behaviour. What is it?

This is probably related to his main character flaw. For example, if he's a coward, he learns to be brave when it counts. If he's prone to impulsive deeds, he learns to think before he acts. If he's prejudiced against aristocrats, he learns that some of them are truly noble.

He may learn this lesson in several parts. At first, he rejects it, or absorbs it only on a superficial level. But in the second half of the book, perhaps during the Black Moment, he finally understands that he must let go of the beliefs that don't serve him, and with this new perspective he takes action, perhaps during the novel's Climax.

Establish his flaw – the one he needs to overcome – early on in the story, and show it several times.

Let's say his flaw is prejudice. His experiences have made him wary of Chinese immigrants. Early in the book, show how he is circumspect in his dealings with Chinese people. Choosing between two shortlisted candidates for an accounts job, and he hires the Native American rather than the Chinese. Presented with a proposal by a Chinese businessman, he gets his lawyer to check the contract extra carefully. When his teenage daughter accepts a date with a Chinese boy, he hires a private investigator to check the boy's background. On its own, none of these actions says 'prejudice', but in combination, they send the signal.

Around the middle of the book, he comes to appreciate one particular Chinese person's integrity, and when his situation is desperate, he turns to the local Chinese community for help. By the end of the story, he has learnt that while some Chinese people are dishonest, others are trustworthy, and he now judges Asians by their deeds rather than their ethnicity.

Keep the flaw subtle. A strong flaw can make readers detest the MC. If the MC refuses to employ any Chinese people, forbids his teenage daughter to go to the prom with a Chinese boy, and if he treats all Chinese with contempt, readers won't like him. Many will stop reading after a few pages and never get to the part where he mends his ways.

Don't let the lesson change the MC into a different person. A 180 degree personality turn is not believable. However, he has become aware of his weakness, gained control over it and modified his behaviour.

What if the MC's tendency to like everyone makes him trust the wrong people, until he learns to become discerning?

What if he always jumps at opportunities, until he learns to investigate them?

What if he falls in love with every blue-eyed freckled blonde until one abuses him so badly that he learns to look behind the face?

What if he believes he is righteous beyond temptation until seduced by an evil schemer?

What if he's convinced that his decisions are best for his family and expects them to submit without complaint, until one of his orders leads to a tragedy?

PLOT REVISION PROMPT:
THE MC'S HIDDEN HOPE

Your main character has a hope, an ambition, a dream... something so personal that she hasn't told anyone. Perhaps she doesn't even admit it to herself, and would deny such crazy aspirations.

Unlike her big goal, the hope is not part of the main plot, though it may be part of the subtext or a subplot. She doesn't consciously set out to achieve this, although she may subconsciously make choices which take her towards this dream.

What if she outwardly denies any affection for her estranged father, but deep down longs for reconciliation with him? What if she doesn't want the work and commitment that comes from adopting a dog, but really longs for a canine companion? What if she proclaims free love without the shackles of marriage, but part of her longs to settle down to a conventional lifestyle with a husband and two point four children?

Hint at this dream repeatedly. Perhaps she can't bring herself to destroy the photo of herself and her dad in happier childhood days. Perhaps she notices the soulful eyes of the neighbour's dog and the playful antics of her friend's puppy. Perhaps her gaze frequently wanders to the young married couple who are obviously content in their marriage.

Gradually, she admits to herself that this is something she wants.

Rouse and dash the hope several times.

At the novel's end, you may want to grant her wish. Your readers will feel deep satisfaction.

PLOT REVISION PROMPT: CREATE A METAPHOR

You may not have used intentional metaphors when you wrote your draft for this novel – but you may have created them without meaning to. These metaphors, not forced but arising naturally, are often the best.

Find one potential metaphor and develop it.

Look for recurring objects, actions, locations.

Perhaps the story features several cellars, several masks, several towers, several demolitions. Pick one of them to use as your story's metaphor.

What symbolic meanings does a cellar, mask, tower, demolition have? Make a list of possible meanings, and choose one that is significant in your story's context.

Perhaps the cellar stands for unseen resources and reserves, the mask for hiding one's true feelings, the tower for ambitions or demolition for the destruction of false hopes.

When you hit on a good metaphor, you'll get a distinct feeling, "Yes, this is perfect for this book."

Now visit all places where that metaphor occurs – all scenes involving a cellar, mask, tower or demolition – and flesh them out a little, tweaking them so that the metaphor's unspoken meaning rings in the subtext.

Keep it so subtle that most readers are only subconsciously aware of the metaphor.

PLOT REVISION PROMPTS: PREPARE FOR THE IMPLAUSIBLE

If something in the plot may strike the reader as difficult to believe, prepare the ground by mentioning it casually beforehand.

Let's say a dinosaur suddenly appears in the second half of the book. Readers will find this implausible unless you have planted earlier hints. Perhaps a minor character is a dinosaur DNA researcher, while another writes a college paper about whether or not dinosaurs are truly extinct.

If a devoted, strictly moral woman in her sixties suddenly leaves her husband to take up with a band of free-loving neo-hippies, this will jar with the reader's perceptions because it's so out of character. It will feel believable, though, if during a conversation early in the book she casually mentions "the wild days of my youth" so the reader is aware of that facet of personality.

What if a volcano eruption suddenly destroys a town? Sure, volcanoes can erupt unexpectedly – but the reader will feel better if there has been a warning hint. Perhaps you can show the lava from an eruption three thousand years ago, or maybe an adult explains to his children that they are quite safe because that volcano is dead, which immediately puts the reader on alert. You could also show columns of smoke rising from the crater, an event so regular that the locals pay scarce attention, although it creates an atmospheric image.

PLOT REVISION PROMPT: USE A TICKING CLOCK

Give the MC a deadline by when to achieve his goal. If he misses the cut-off point, the consequences will be terrible.

Let's say the MC is a homicide detective hunting a serial killer who ritually slaughters a child in every full moon night. She has to hunt him down before the next full moon, or another child will die.

Perhaps her goal is to prove that it wasn't her brother who robbed the stagecoach and killed the passengers. She has to find the real criminal before the day of the execution, or her brother will be hanged.

If she is determined to protect her sister from marrying a bigamist, she needs to track down the scoundrel's existing wife before the wedding.

As secret agent, she needs to find the location of the villain's lair containing the trigger which will launch a nuclear war – and she knows the trigger is set to go off in ten days.

Throughout the novel, remind the reader of the deadline, and show how the time is passing. For example, you can describe the moon in every chapter of the book, showing how it waxes from a thin crescent to a gibbous disk, filling out further every night. You can count the days until the nuclear meltdown, or display the wedding preparations. A real clock or a calendar can also serve well.

The closer the deadline gets, the greater the suspense. Readers will hold their breath while the MC races against the clock.

Make the most of this tension. Allow the MC to succeed in the last moment, with not a minute to spare.

PLOT REVISION PROMPT: SET SCENES

Your readers have been waiting for certain scenes. The characters talked about a forthcoming event, the tension about it is high. How will things turn out? When the reader finally reaches the scene, she wants to get a major experience.

These scenes are 'set scenes' and your novel probably contains several. They include the lovers confessing their feelings, the first confrontation between hero and villain, and the final showdown, as well as anything the characters are anticipating.

Let's say you've written historical novel about the Alaska goldrush. Your MC is certain he'll strike gold in a certain location, and he overcomes many obstacles to stake his claim, obtain equipment, keep his secret. The moment he sees the first glint of gold you have a set scene.

Some fiction genres have traditional set scenes because of the reader's expectations. These include the heroine's coming-out ball in a Historical Romance, the sword duel in a Sword'n'Sorcery Fantasy, the MC captured by and escaping the serial killer in a Thriller, and the shootout in a Western.

If your Historical Romance contains a coming-out ball, you'd better describe it in lavish detail, or your readers will be disappointed.

How do you do this? First, make sure you develop a complete scene. Don't just throw down a few summary sentences *(The ball went well, and Mary danced with many eligible bachelors, although Mr Handsome did not propose.)* or skip this important part altogether. *(After months of hardship, John sensed he would find gold here, and he dug with fervour. Later, when he showed the found lumps of ore at the bank...)*

The set scene should be as long as, or longer than, the average scene in your book.

Conjure up lavish details with sensory descriptions. In the Alaska goldmine, let the reader hear the sounds of the pickaxe and smell the odours under ground. Devote a whole paragraph to describing that first glint of gold. For the coming-out ball, describe the ballroom floor, the dresses of the ladies, the scents of the flower decorations, and how the MC's feet feel after dancing for three hours in her new slippers.

Shift important conflicts and revelations so they take place in this scene to add drama and tension. Make this the scene when the MC discovers that his buddy is a convicted murderer recently escaped from jail, or when Mr Handsome confesses that he is betrothed to someone else.

Refine the dialogue so it sparkles with diamond brilliance.

Put obstacles in the MC's way. Don't let John find the gold easily and rejoice in his discovery without opposition, or permit Mary to enjoy her coming-out ball without problems.

PLOT REVISION PROMPT: INNER CONFLICT

What does your MC most want? This is probably her goal in this novel.

What is the exact opposite of that? Make her want this as well. Give her a good reason for this desire.

Does she acknowledge this need to others? Does she even acknowledge it to herself? What inner turmoil does this create – confusion, yearning, guilt?

In what scenes can this conflict play out?

PLOT REVISION PROMPT: SHOW THE MC'S HEROIC QUALITY IN CHAPTER 1

Readers like main characters who are stronger and braver than themselves. Find a way to show (not tell) this at the novel's start.

What if a minor emergency arises, and the MC takes charge, keeps a cool head while everyone around her panics, and directs the rescue?

You can show the MC doing her day-to-day job with an efficiency the reader will admire, or you can show her reacting with gumption to an unexpected event.

Emphasise this heroic quality by contrasting it with the behaviour of other people in the scene. Perhaps a crowd gathers around the scene of an accident, and while the others wail about how terrible the person's injuries are, the MC kneels down and applies skilled first aid. Or maybe a child is stuck in the railings of a fourth floor balcony and may fall any moment. Others gape in horror while the MC climbs up to rescue the kid.

As long as you keep the act within the realms of plausibility, readers will believe the event and love your MC. Deep down, they wish to be like this.

PLOT REVISION PROMPT: THE MC'S REACTION IS NOT WHAT EVERYONE EXPECTS

Pick a section in your draft where something unexpected happens.

Let your MC react and act differently from everyone else.

Are all other characters furious about what just occurred? The MC is laid back and views the event with humour.

Is everyone confident and raring to go? The MC displays scepticism and caution.

This will make your MC more interesting to the reader.

For best effect, show the reason for the MC's stance, but don't dwell on it. A few words are enough.

PLOT REVISION PROMPT: IRREVOCABLE COMMITMENT

Pick a moment in your novel where the MC makes or renews his commitment to the cause. Flesh out this scene.

Show the MC's motivation. Why does he make this commitment? Why does he make it now? Is it a spontaneous act, or something he has considered for a long time?

Later in the novel, this commitment will be severely tested, and the reader will feel the greatest anguish on the MC's behalf if she has come to share the commitment.

PLOT REVISION PROMPT: NO TURNING BACK

Find the moment in your draft where the MC realises that there is no turning back. In some novels, this is also the moment of irrevocable commitment, and it is probably one of the turning points.

Write a paragraph about this realisation. For best effect, blend actions with reactions, events with thoughts.

This is a dramatic moment, and your readers deserve the best you can give.

PLOT REVISION PROMPT: AVOID AN OVER-USED BEGINNING

Most novels submitted by new writers begin with one of these:

1. The MC wakes up and gets ready for the day.

2. The MC stands in front of her wardrobe and contemplates what to wear for an upcoming event.

3. The MC gazes out of the window and reflects on her past and future.

4. The MC sits in a bar or restaurant, waiting for someone to arrive.

5. The MC walks, drives or rides to a place where she expects to meet someone or do something.

If your draft begins with one of these, try a different start. In many cases, the draft's second chapter can become the final version's opening.

PLOT REVISION PROMPT: ADDITIONAL PROBLEMS

Consider the MC's main goal in this story. What other problems does he have relating to this goal? Make a list. Use these complications to enrich the plot and deepen the story.

PLOT REVISION PROMPT: USE YOUR PERSONAL EXPERIENCE

Have you been in similar situations as the MC? Perhaps you, too, have adopted a rescue dog, suffered a bereavement, succumbed to temptation, endured an abusive relationship, raised funds for a campaign, won a grant, arrived late for an appointment, dressed wrongly for a crucial occasion, said something really stupid in a job interview?

Make a list – the longer, the better.

Revive those moments in your mind. Call up how you felt, how you acted, how the other people behaved. The more details you can recall, the better. The scratchy dryness of your throat when you tried to talk, the squeaky sound of your voice, the thudding of your heart, how the interviewer rolled his eyes and shuffled his papers, the way you kept finding excuses for your partner's violence and blaming yourself...

Find ways to incorporate those details into your story. Make your experiences the MC's experiences.

SCENE REVISION PROMPTS

Here you'll find ideas to transform dull, dragging scenes into riveting reads with tension and sizzle.

SCENE REVISION PROMPT: CHANGE THE LOCATION

To make a scene more interesting, move it to an unusual location. Far too many scenes take place in restaurants, bars and boardrooms. Shift yours to a swimming pool, a skiing slope or a storage shed, and the reader's interest will perk up.

If the scene is based on a planned meeting, think of ways how you could force them to relocate at short notice.

What if the executives had planned to meet in the boardroom as usual, but a burst water pipe makes it impossible, so they have to gather in the laboratory?

What if the young people are about to order their meal during their first date, when the restaurant gets evacuated because of a bomb alert, and they have to huddle on a bench in a nearby bus shelter while they wait to be allowed back in?

To make the most of the location, convey sensory impressions – the smell of chlorine in the swimming pool, the dim light coming through the crack in the shed's wall – and let the characters interact with the environment – sitting at the pool edge with their feet dangling in the water, or stomping uphill with every step sinking deep into the snow.

SCENE REVISION PROMPT: KEEPING SECRETS

One of the characters – either the MC or one of the others – has a secret. This can be something he needs to hide at all cost, or simply something he'd rather not expose at this stage.

How does he avoid the subject or deny the fact in dialogue?

Are the other characters probing?

Does one of them suspect the truth?

From whom in particular does the character wish to hide the secret, and why?

Does the reader know the secret yet?

Consider using body language (avoided eye contact, small gestures with arms close to the body) to hint at the secret. This works best if the secret holder is not the scene's Point-of-View character.

SCENE REVISION PROMPT: STATE THE GOAL

What does the MC want to achieve in this scene? If it's a meeting, perhaps she wants to persuade or convince the others of something. If it's an action scene, she may want to defeat an opponent, hunt down a fugitive, escape a villain's clutches or lift treasure out of shark-infested waters.

This scene goal is probably in some way related to the novel goal, and may even be part of it, but it doesn't have to be.

State the goal early in the scene, and repeat it in different ways. You can simply tell the reader what it is, for example: *She had to get across the moat before the guards discovered her absence.* You can use questions: *How could she get across the moat?* The character's thoughts are another possibility, although it's best to keep them brief: *I must get across the moat.* If the scene involves more than one character, use dialogue. *"I must get across the moat. Can you watch out for the guards?"*

Use different words each time you state the scene goal.

Giving the MC a specific goal to achieve will create a hook. Now the reader wants to know if and how the MC achieves success.

To create excitement, give the MC a limited time to achieve the scene goal:

What if she needs to get across the moat before the villain returns home? She has a twenty-minute window to make her escape from the castle, and has already spent ten minutes on getting out of the keep.

What if she needs to get across the moat before the guards reach her? She can already hear their shouts, steps and clanking armour.

What if she needs to get across the moat before the sun sets and the vampires come out? Already the horizon is turning purple with the final rays of the day.

Put several obstacles in the character's way to make it difficult for her to achieve her goal.

SCENE REVISION PROMPT: SWITCH THE POINT OF VIEW

If the scene doesn't work as well as it should, consider changing the PoV. Could you tell it from a different character's perspective?

The ideal PoV

- is present throughout the whole scene
- has a goal or agenda to achieve during the scene
- has a stake in the outcome
- interacts with other characters
- takes action (does something other than watch)

A change of PoV often brings a bland scene to life.

SCENE REVISION PROMPT: EVERYONE HAS AN AGENDA

To create tension in a scene, give every character an agenda. Each wants to achieve something, whether that's small or large, whether or not they tell the others about it.

The reader doesn't need to be consciously aware of everyone's agenda, only that of the two or three main characters.

What if one character wants to gain information about the other guy's plans?

What if one aims to provoke the other into a fight?

What if the waitress wants to earn a big tip?

Give every character an agenda, and the scene will suddenly sizzle.

SCENE REVISION PROMPT: WHAT'S THE WEATHER LIKE?

Weather creates mood and atmosphere, and it affects how people move and feel. Give the scene specific weather. What's the weather like in the region where your story takes place at that time of the year? Rain or drought? Heat or cold? Sweltering heat or biting cold? Could there be a thunderstorm, a blizzard, a hurricane?

The weather and temperature affect the pace and purpose of movement – for the scene's acting characters as well as for the bystanders. In cold weather, they'll move fast, with their hands in their pockets, and they won't linger. They may rub their hands, stomp their feet or hug themselves for warmth. In hot weather, movements are slow and languid, and most people seek the shade of walls or trees. When it rains, they move fast, usually leaning forward with their heads bent.

If your scene is set out of doors, describe how the weather affects the point of view character:

Does the cold wind sting her cheeks? Is sweat trickling from her armpits? Has the rain plastered the skirt to her thighs?

In a long scene, you can create extra interest by intensifying or changing the weather. What if the drizzle turns into a downpour? What if the wind picks up and grows into a gale?

For an indoor scene, the weather plays a lesser role, but you can still use it. Focus on sounds: Is the wind whining in the chimney and rattling the shutters? Do raindrops patter against the window pane? Does the ceiling-fan whirr?

SCENE REVISION PROMPT:
ADD BACKGROUND NOISES

What sounds characterise the location where this scene takes place? Are there blackbirds twittering or seagulls screeching? Might there be a dog's bark or a coyote's howl in the distance? Maybe cars hum past, a door slams, a water pipe gurgles in the wall?

Sounds add atmosphere as well as excitement. Insert several sentences into your scene at different points.

The best places to insert a background sound are:

- when there's a silence or pregnant pause in the dialogue

- when the PoV character is waiting for something

- in moments of suspense when you want to turn the tension up even more

SCENE REVISION PROMPT: ADD SMELLS

Smells, more than any other sensual impression, pull the reader into a story. As soon as you mention a smell, your readers experience the scene as if they were there.

Smells also characterise places, people and objects more than visual descriptions can.

What does the room smell like? Of beer and unwashed socks? Of cannabis and patchouli? Of beeswax and lavender? Of bleach and chemical lemon?

What does a character smell like? Of fresh sweat and leather? Of stale sweat and cigarette smoke? Of wood and freshly mown grass? Of Brylcream and coal tar soap? Is there a hint of rose fragrance, or does she smell as if she had drenched her clothes in a whole bottle of rose perfume?

Describe the smell of the old documents, the wine, the paint or whatever the scene's Point-of-View character gets close to.

The best place to mention odours and scents is when the PoV experiences them for the first time, for example, when he enters the room, shakes hands with the stranger, opens the box.

SCENE REVISION PROMPT:
ADD ACTION TO DIALOGUE

Give your characters something to do while they talk. This avoids bland 'Talking Heads' scenes.

Engage them a in routine chore – mowing the lawn, washing the dishes – or better still, give them a task which relates to the scene goal or the story goal. Keep them busy digging a tunnel, hoisting the sails, gathering wood for a signal fire.

SCENE REVISION PROMPT: CUT THE JOURNEY

In your draft, the scene may have a slow start. The MC walks, drives or rides to the place where the action happens.

Authors like to begin scenes this way, because it allows them to get into the scene gradually, like a warm-up exercise. But for the reader, this is dull. Cut the journey, including all the memories and contemplations going through the MC's head.

Instead, start when the MC arrives at the place, just before he opens the door... or even when he is already there.

SCENE REVISION PROMPT: WALKING THROUGH THE DOOR

Add suspense to your scene by letting the MC enter through a door or gateway. This works best if the scene involves a dangerous experience, not for everyday pleasant events.

The 'door' moment can happen near the beginning of the scene (if there has been a build-up to the experience) or in the middle. The readers should already feel a bit wary, and the doorway is a psychological trick to ratchet up their suspense.

Something inside them screams, "Don't open that door!" Of course the MC does open it, and the readers sit on the edge of their chair, biting their nails in anticipation.

Slow the pace while the MC opens the door. Describe what it looks like - the imposing arch and the big brass bell, the splintered wood and peeling paint, the barbed wire and 'Keep Out – Danger!' sign. Delay the MC while he gropes for the key in his pocket, inserts and turns it. Describe the noises of the door opening. Does it screech, whine, whirr?

To increase the tension to maximum volume, describe the sound of the door closing behind the MC. Whether it clicks shut or slams shut, the readers now have the feeling that the MC has walked into a trap. This technique works especially well for thrillers and horror fiction.

SCENE REVISION PROMPT:
MIX UP THE SENSES

Most writers, when creating the first draft for a story, focus on just one sense – vision. They describe what the character sees.

However, other senses create stronger impressions, and make the scene more vivid. Aim to use three or more senses in every scene.

Here are the main senses to choose from:

Vision – what the PoV character sees. Most writers find this sense the easiest to use. Unfortunately, it's the least exciting, and on its own can be dull.

Sound – what the PoV character hears. This sense creates excitement and suspense, and is suitable for all scenes.

Smell - what the PoV character smells. This sense is the most evocative. It suits most scenes, but only when the PoV first notices the odour, e.g. on entering a room.

Touch – what the PoV character feels when touching something. This not just about her hands, but can include the surfaces she walks, stands or lies on, leans against, or bumps into, as well as what she experiences when something or someone touches her. In erotic scenes as well as scenes set in total darkness, this sense should play a major role.

Taste – what the PoV character tastes with her tongue. This suits mostly those scenes in which she eats or drinks. She may also taste blood (if she's been injured in a fight) or bile.

Humans have many more senses, so don't restrict yourself to just the five main ones. The following senses can be highly effective in some scenes:

Temperature – when the PoV feels warm or cold. This sense works for many scenes in all genres. It can serve to convey, emphasise or intensify emotions such as discomfort and fear.

Pain - when the PoV is physically hurting. This may be related to the sense of touch - for example, she touches the hotplate, her finger hurts for a while afterwards – but it can also be unrelated, such as a migraine or stomach cramps.

Balance – what helps the PoV character stay upright. Humans aren't normally aware of this unless the balance is off, which leads to dizziness and perhaps nausea.

Try to use at least three different senses in every scene.

SCENE REVISION PROMPT: INCREASE SUSPENSE

At the scene's most suspenseful moment – when the story's characters and your readers are waiting with bated breath to find out what will happen next, slow the pace.

Do this by focusing on a detail, something small and probably unconnected to the issue, that the Point-of-View character is likely to notice: the cobweb in the corner of the ceiling, the grease stain on the table cloth, the lizard sunbathing on the garden wall, the purple varnish on the other woman's nails.

Small visual details work well, as do background noises. Other senses may not be as effective here.

SCENE REVISION PROMPT: ACTION SOUNDS

Whatever the characters do probably creates sounds. Let the reader hear the resulting noises, because sounds create excitement.

Swords clank. Fists thud on flesh. Cutlery scrapes on plates. Glasses chink. Keyboards click.

SCENE REVISION PROMPT: DEFY EXPECTATIONS

The MC and other characters have entered the scene with expectations of what will happen – something they hope for, or something they fear.

Make sure that events don't play out as the characters expect. Let things get much better or much worse, and throw unexpected twists into the mix.

Consider the reader's expectations, too. If you've built up to an important scene – the marriage proposal in a Romance, the bank robbery in a Western, the confrontation with the serial killer in a Thriller – the reader's expectations are high. Don't disappoint the reader – but don't give her what she expects either. Give her something more moving, more hilarious, more exciting, more devastating.

SCENE REVISION PROMPT: DENIAL

One of the characters – perhaps the MC – isn't ready to acknowledge something to himself. What is it? Are the other characters aware of it? If yes, do they try to open his eyes to the truth? How does he react?

SCENE REVISION PROMPT: DIALOGUE

To make dialogue more exciting, phrase much of it as questions rather than statements.

Instead of
I can't find my money.
Consider
Have you seen my money?

Instead of
The bridge may collapse.
Consider
What if the bridge collapses?

To make dialogue sizzle with tension, use questions answered with questions:

"Who was this woman just now?"
"Why do you want to know?"
"Why don't you tell me who she is and what she wanted from you?"
"Why are you so obsessed with her?"

By rephrasing several statements as questions, you can make your dialogue sparkle.

SCENE REVISION PROMPT: ACTING 'IN CHARACTER'

Pick a character in the scene you want to revise – either the MC or someone else. Consider this person's main character traits and choose one.

Find ways to emphasise this character trait in the scene.

Could she talk differently, use different body language, make a different choice, show a different attitude?

Let's say one of this character's defining attitudes is impatience. To emphasise this, show her glancing at her watch, tapping her fingers, cutting another character's speech short, suggesting shortcuts, rolling her eyes when someone goes on and on, and being the first out of the door.

SCENE REVISION PROMPT: CREATE A 'ZINGER'

A 'zinger' is a pithy one-liner. In just a few words, the character expresses not just meaning, but attitude.

Readers love dialogue zingers. Try to create them, especially for the book's main characters.

Choose a dialogue section where the character says something witty, devastating or provocative. Shave off every word that's not absolutely necessary, until the bare essence remains. Now replace dull words with short vivid ones. Voilà – you have a zinger.

Create at least one zinger in every dialogue, especially near the end of the exchange. You can use several. When hero and villain sling zingers at each other, or hero and heroine banter with zingers, the scene sizzles.

SCENE REVISION PROMPT: LOCATION RESEARCH

Visit a place that's similar to the scene's setting.

Does the scene feature a brawl in a wild west saloon bar? Go and have a drink in a pub. Does your Chicklit heroine shop for shoes in Harrod's in London? Visit a local shoe shop. Are pirates boarding the frigate? Book a tour of a historical replica sailing vessel. Does your MC get attacked by muggers in a dark inner city alleyway at night? Go for a walk in the dark in your home town – but stay safe.

You'll probably not be able to visit a location that's exactly like that in your book. As long as it has some similarities, you'll find it inspiring. Observe and take notes of background noises, smells, people's behaviour, body language, overheard snatches of conversation and anything else you can use. Then adapt these details and weave them into your scene.

SCENE REVISION PROMPT:
A MEDLEY OF EMOTIONS

What emotions does the Point-of-View character feel in this scene? In the draft version, he may have just one emotion.

Layer the emotions, so he feels several at once, and vary them, so the feelings differ during different parts of the scene.

Perhaps he starts with apprehension and curiosity. The apprehension gives way to fascination, while the curiosity stays. Then surprise replaces them both. A moment later, he feels disbelief with gradually building resentment. The resentment gradually builds into anger, yet at the same time he feels pride because he has discovered the truth.

Identify what he feels at what stage. Now find ways of expressing these emotions – preferably by showing, not telling.

SCENE REVISION PROMPT: INCREASE THE VOLUME

Make the funny bits in your scene funnier, the shocking revelations more shocking, the romantic elements more wildly romantic, the vulgar dialogue more vulgar. Whatever channels the reader is tuning into, turn up the volume.

These changes can relate to actions, dialogue, setting, behaviour or anything else. Find at least five ways to increase the volume of something in this scene.

DEEPEN THE POINT-OF-VIEW

In your draft, you've probably written everything the way you would experience it. But the scene's Point-of-View character (who is probably the MC) has a different background and therefore different perceptions.

What would she really hear, see, smell and think?

Consider her reactions to other people. Let's say she's a safety-obsessed perfectionist. When strolling in the rose garden, would her attention truly be on the blooms, or would she notice uneven flagstones?

Find five or more spots where you can tweak something to reflect the PoV character's background and personality.

SCENE REVISION PROMPT:
CREATE AN END-OF-SCENE HOOK

At the end of your scene, hook your reader so he simply needs to read on.

The best way to achieve this is to put a question in the reader's mind: What will happen next? Who is the murderer? How can the MC escape? How is she going to solve this dilemma? Will Mr Handsome propose marriage? Does this mine shaft lead to gold? Can John be trusted?

Here are four techniques:

1. State the MC's goal for the next scene. While she recovers from the events of this scene, she makes a resolution: *Tomorrow was her last chance to snare a husband. She had to find a way to get John to propose.*

2. Create a cliffhanger. The MC is in a precarious situation of acute danger when the chapter ends. The reader can't wait to find out what happens next, so he turns the page and starts the next chapter. Often, the cliffhanger doesn't really end the scene. Rather, a long scene spreads across two chapters. The cliffhanger serves to connect the two. *With all her remaining strength, Mary hung on to the rock. Her fingers grew numb, and the ground beneath her feet crumbled.*

3. End the scene so the MC is in a worse situation than before. Whatever her goal was at the beginning of the scene, she not only failed to achieve it, but her efforts landed her in greater trouble. *Mary dug her nails into her palms as she replayed the interview in her mind. Instead of convincing Mr John that she was a competent businesswoman, she had given the impression of being a crook. Now she would never get the loan! What could she do?*

4. Near the end of the scene, introduce an unexpected obstacle to the MC's big goal. Let's say Mary wants to marry John – that's her big story goal. Her goal for this scene was to get invited to his home. She achieves this, but there's a big 'but'.
   "You're a natural diplomat, Mary," John said. "Will you do me a favour and come to tea tomorrow? Break it to them that I'm going to marry Lady Louisa. If it comes from you, it will be less of a shock."

LINE EDITING PROMPTS

Before you indie-publish your book or submit it to agents, enhance your style with sharp writing and a strong voice, where every word pulls the reader in. The polishing prompts help make your book sparkle with diamond quality.

LINE EDITING PROMPT:
THE THREE MOST OVER-USED SENTENCES

Almost all manuscripts by novice writers contain these three sentences, often more than once:

He/she turned to look at him/her.
He/she nodded slowly.
He/she took a deep breath to steady himself/herself.

Scour your draft for those sentences, including minor variations, and kill them. Either replace them with something more original, or simply leave them out.

LINE EDITING PROMPT: DELETE FILLER WORDS

Certain words hold no real meaning and can almost always be deleted:

really
completely
absolutely
totally
rather
quite

You may want to use your word processor's 'find' function to hunt them down. In most cases, you can simply cut them.

The earthquake was really very terrible, and it totally destroyed the whole town.

Without the filler words, this sentence becomes:

The earthquake was terrible, and it destroyed the whole town. (This sentence is not an example of brilliant writing, just an illustration how filler words can be cut without loss of meaning.)

Without filler words, your writing becomes leaner, faster paced and more interesting to read.

LINE EDITING PROMPT: GET RID OF TAUTOLOGIES

Some sentences in your draft may be saying the same things over: *cold ice, hot fire, white snow, black coal.* Delete the unnecessary word.

Tautologies often creep in when body parts move:

He nodded his head.
She shrugged her shoulders.
He blinked his eyes.

Since 'shrug' implies shoulders, 'nod' head and 'blink' eyes, you can simply write:

He nodded.
She shrugged.
He blinked.

On the other hand, if the character nods, shrugs or blinks a different body part, that would be worth mentioning!

LINE EDITING PROMPT: CUT THE 'COULD'

Whenever your draft tells the reader that the MC could hear, could see, could feel, could sense or could smell something, let him hear, see, feel, sense or smell it instead. Simply cut the word 'could'.

Could hear > heard
could see > saw
could feel > felt
could taste > tasted
could sense > sensed
could smell > smelled

Your wordprocessing software has a 'find' or 'search' function. Use it to highlight every 'could' in your draft, so you can see at a glance where they are.

For even stronger writing, consider if you can cut the *hear, see, feel, smell, sense* as well. Often you can, especially if you've established the PoV clearly. Then you don't need to say that the PoV character hears the sounds, smells the smells and sees the visions.

Example:

The sentence
She could hear the back gate squeal.
Becomes
She heard the back gate squeal.
Or
The back gate squealed.

LINE EDITING PROMPT:
CUT UNNEEDED 'SAID'

Dialogue tags – such as *he said, she replied* - are often unnecessary.

If they serve no purpose, delete them.

Before:
"Please stay with me," she pleaded, clasping his hand.
"I'm sorry, I can't. I have to go," he said and rose from his chair.

After:
She clasped his hand. "Please stay with me."
"I'm sorry, I can't. I have to go." He rose from his chair.

Keep dialogue tags only if they aid clarity. Some tags make it easier for the reader to follow who is saying what. Don't delete those.

LINE EDITING PROMPT:
VIVID VERBS NEED NO ADVERBS

Adverbs add meaning to a verb. If you choose the right verbs, you won't need adverbs. Lots of adverbs are a sign of sloppy writing.

Go through your draft and consider every adverb: could it be redundant if you changed the verb?

He shouted loudly. > He yelled.
She ran quickly. > She raced.
He turned instantly. > He spun.
She walked happily down the stairs. > She bounced down the stairs.
He touched her hand tenderly. > He caressed her hand.

You don't need to kill every adverb in your manuscript. Simply reduce their number.

LINE EDITING PROMPT: HOW TO CONVEY TEDIUM

If the MC finds something boring or tedious, you need to convey that – but without boring the reader! Here's a nifty technique.

Find a spot where the MC is engaged in a tedious task or has to observe boring repetitions.

Create a sentence based on a list with all items linked with the word 'and':

While the young ladies sat on the verandah sipping tea, Ann had to wash the dishes and launder the linen and dust the furniture and scrub the floors.

The politician droned on about how his party would protect liberty and create jobs and reduce crime and support education and regenerate the economy.

This creates a sense of tedium... but since it's just one sentence, the reader won't find it tedious to read.

This technique is best used sparingly, no more than once or twice per chapter.

LINE EDITING PROMPT:
HOW TO CONVEY SPEEDY ACTION

Find a section in your draft where things happen, perhaps when the MC carries out several actions in rapid succession.

Create a sentence with a list of words – either nouns or verbs – and present them without 'and' or other link words, just with commas.

Examples:

He thrust, parried, slashed.

She grabbed coins, credit cards, jewellery, laptop, anything that looked valuable.

This creates a sense of breathlessness and speed.

LINE EDITING PROMPT:
REMOVE BARRIER WORDS

Certain words create a barrier between the reader and the story experience: see, notice, realise, observe, watch, wonder, think.

Remove as many as possible from your manuscript.

She realised that the exit was blocked. >> The exit was blocked. She saw the men labour and sweat under the searing sun > The men laboured and sweated under the searing sun.

Removing barrier words (also called 'filter words') gives the reader a more direct, intense experience.

Some barrier words provide a useful service, for example, to indicate a change of Point of View. Keep those.

LINE EDITING PROMPT:
VARY THE BODY LANGUAGE

First drafts often contain a limited body language vocabulary. The characters always sigh, nod, shrug, shake their heads, clench their fists, bite their lips and raise their brows.

Find instances in your manuscript where you've used these and think of different body language cues to express the characters' reactions.

LINE EDITING PROMPT: REDUCING THE INGINGINGS

Early drafts are often littered with words ending in 'ing'. These include:

- Gerunds (verbs used as nouns). Example: *The **exploring** came to an **ending.***

- Present participles (a verb about what's happening at the moment of speaking). Example: ***Clutching** her purse, Mary raced down the road, **panting** for breath.*

There's nothing wrong with gerunds or present participles, or with any other 'ing'-ending word. But when many of them cluster closely together, as they often do in drafts, they create a clumsy style: ***Understanding** that **creating** immediacy is **something** important in **writing, beginning** writers often make the mistake of **using** too many present participles, often **adding** other words also **ending** in 'ing', without **realising** the effect those are **having.***

Check your draft, and rephrase any sections with too many 'ing'-words.

LINE EDITING PROMPT: HOLD THE BREATHS

Many drafts have a surfeit of breathing, breath-drawing, breath-holding, inhaling and exhaling:

She drew a deep breath.
He took a deep breath to steady himself.
She exhaled slowly.
He inhaled sharply.
She held her breath.
He gasped.

Let your characters inhale and exhale as much as they want to, but don't write it down every time they do.

As you revise your manuscript, delete any surplus breathing announcements.

LINE EDITING PROMPT: USE SMILES SPARINGLY

When their fingers fly across the keyboard, many authors write 'he smiled', 'she smiled' a lot. In real life, seeing lots of smiles around us is lovely, but in fiction, all this smiling soon gets tedious for the reader.

Check your draft. If smiles appear on almost every page, edit most of them out.

Keep only the significant ones, and if possible, express them with different phrases to make them more interesting:

The corners of his eyes crinkled.
Her lips curved with malice.

LINE EDITING PROMPT:
VARY THE SENTENCE BEGINNING

If all sentences begin with the sentence subject *(I... You... He... She... The man... The tree... A car... Two towers... A group of soldiers...)* the resulting rhythm is monotonous.

Avoid starting many sentences in a row with the subject. Give at least every fourth sentence a different beginning.

If you're stuck for ideas, try opening a sentence with the time *(In the evening... At half past four... When the sun rose... As soon as they reached the city gate... Before he could ask...)* or the place *(In Berlin... On the horizon... Across the road... Close to the city wall... Below the tower... On the fifth floor...In his heart... In her hand...)*

LINE EDITING PROMPT:
CUT 'START TO' AND 'BEGIN TO'

Most writers' drafts are riddled with either 'start to' or 'begin to' - or both:

She started to run.
The wind started to pick up.
He began to wonder.
The crowd began to thin.

These can almost always be cut without loss, and the sentence will be tighter and stronger:

She ran.
The wind picked up.
He wondered.
The crowd thinned.

Keep 'begin to' and 'start to' only where they add meaning, for example if a character starts an action and then abandons it.

LINE EDITING PROMPT: REPLACE GENERIC WORDS

Whenever you come across a generic word in your draft, replace it with a specific one.

Here are examples of generic words: tree, building, shoes, flower, move, vehicle. They do their job in the manuscript, but they don't do it well. Specific words, on the other hand, create a clear image in the reader's mind.

Compare these:

Generic: *a row of trees.*
Specific: *a row of poplars, a row of palms, a row of saplings.*

Generic: *a building*
Specific: *a cottage, a tower, a block of flats, a brownstone, a bungalow.*

Generic: *a cat*
Specific: *a tabby, a kitten, a Siamese.*

Generic: *a pair of shoes*
Specific: *a pair of boots, a pair of loafers, a pair of sandals, a pair of slippers, a pair of Manolo Blahniks.*

LINE EDITING PROMPT: BACKLOAD SENTENCES

When editing your manuscript, restructure some sentences so they end with a powerful word.

Sentences closing with words like *love, dead, hurt, child, now, hope, God* leave a stronger impact on the reader's mind than those ending with *then, them, us, about, for, up, it.*

Here's an example:

I fear a divorce is the only option left under the circumstances. I fear the only option left under the circumstances is divorce.

This technique is called 'backloading' and it works especially well for the last sentence of each paragraph.

Try to close many paragraphs with a backloaded sentence – and definitely apply this technique to the last sentence of every scene for lasting impact.

DEAR READER,

I hope you enjoyed this book and have gained many practical ideas how to empower your novel.

I'd love it if you could post a review on Amazon or some other book site where you have an account and posting privileges. Maybe you can mention what kind of fiction you write, and which of the prompts suggested in this guide inspired you most.

Email me the link to your review, and I'll send you a free review copy (ebook) of one of my other *Writer's Craft* books. Let me know which one you would like: *Writing Fight Scenes, Writing Scary Scenes, The Word-Loss Diet, Writing About Magic, Writing About Villains, Writing Dark Stories, Euphonics For Writers, Writing Short Stories to Promote Your Novels, Twitter for Writers, SWOT for Writing Success, Why Does My Book Not Sell? 20 Simple Fixes, Writing Vivid Settings, How To Train Your Cat To Promote Your Book, Writing Deep Point of View, Getting Book Reviews, Writing Vivid Dialogue.*

My email is raynehall00000@gmail.com. Also drop me a line if you've spotted any typos which have escaped the proofreader's eagle eyes, or want to give me private feedback or have questions.

You can also contact me on Twitter: https://twitter.com/RayneHall. Tweet me that you've read this book, and I'll probably follow you back.

The cat cartoons are by Marvin Alonso, Hanna-Riikka and Srijit.

If you find this book helpful, it would be great if you could spread the word about it. Maybe you know other writers who would benefit.

At the end of this book, you'll find an excerpt from another Writer's Craft Guide, *Writing Deep Point of View.* I hope you enjoy it.

With best wishes for your novel and your writing career,

Rayne Hall

EXCERPT: WRITING DEEP POINT OF VIEW

CHAPTER 1: FRESH PERSPECTIVES

Instead of explaining Point of View, I'll let you experience it. Let's do a quick practical exercise.

Wherever you are right now, look out of the window (or step out into the open, or do whatever comes closest). If possible, open the window and stick your head out. What do you notice?

Return to your desk or notebook, and jot down two sentences about your spontaneous observations.

You can jot down anything—the cars rushing by, the rain-heavy clouds drawing up on the horizon, the scent of lilacs, the wasps buzzing around the dumpster, the aeroplane scratching the sky, the empty beer cans in the gutter, the rain-glistening road, whatever. Don't bother writing beautiful prose—only the content matters. And only two sentences.

When you've done this—but not before—read on.

*

*

*

Have you written two sentences about what you observed outside the window? Good. Now we'll have fun.

Imagine that you're a different person. Pick one of these:

1. A 19-year-old female student, art major, currently planning to create a series of paintings of townscapes, keenly aware of colours and shapes.

2. A professional musician with sharp ears and a keen sense of rhythm.

3. An eighty-year-old man with painful arthritic knees which get worse in cold weather. He's visiting his daughter and disapproves of the place where she's living these days.

4. A retired health and safety inspector.

5. An architect whose hobby is local history.

6. A hobby gardener with a keen sense of smell.

7. A security consultant assessing the place where a foreign royal princess is going to walk among the people next week.

Once again, stick your head out of the window. What do you notice this time? Return to your desk and jot down two sentences.

I bet the observations are very different! Each time, you saw, heard and smelled the same place—but the first time you experienced it as yourself (from your Point of View) and the second time, as a fictional character (from that character's PoV).

You may want to repeat this exercise with another character from the list, to deepen your insight and practice the skill. If you're an eager learner, do all seven. This will give you a powerful understanding of how PoV works.

Now let's take it one step further: Imagine you're the main character from the story you're currently writing (or have recently finished). How would he experience this place? What would he notice above all else? Again, write two sentences.

Now you've experienced the power of PoV, this is how you will write all your fiction.

ASSIGNMENT

Repeat this exercise in a different place—perhaps when you have time to kill during a train journey or in the dentist's waiting room.

Printed in Great Britain
by Amazon